Do Police Abuse
Their Powers?

William Dudley

ReferencePoint
Press®

San Diego, CA

About the Author
William Dudley is a substitute teacher and writer whose YA nonfiction books for teen readers include *Biofuels* and *Unicorns*. He has a BA in English from Beloit College, Wisconsin.

© 2017 ReferencePoint Press, Inc.
Printed in the United States

For more information, contact:
ReferencePoint Press, Inc.
PO Box 27779
San Diego, CA 92198
www.ReferencePointPress.com

Picture Credits:

Cover: iStockphoto.com
6: Shutterstock.com/AAraujo
10: Joe Raedle/Getty Images
13: Thinkstock Images
17: Associated Press
23: Shutterstock.com/Rena Schild
25: Depositphotos
29: iStockphoto.com
34: Scott Olson/Getty Images
37: Shutterstock.com/Zoran Karapancev
40: Andrew Burton/Getty Images
45: Associated Press
49: Win McNamee/Getty Images
52: Damon Higgins/Zuma Press/Newscom
55: Scott Olson/Getty Images
59: Alex Wong/Getty Images
63: Associated Press

LIBRARY OF CONGRESS CATALOGING-IN-PUBLICATION DATA

Names: Dudley, William, 1964- author.
Title: Do police abuse their powers? / by William Dudley.
Description: San Diego, CA : ReferencePoint Press, Inc., 2017. |
  Series: Issues in society | Includes bibliographical references and index.
Identifiers: LCCN 2016013749 (print) | LCCN 2016021388 (ebook) | ISBN
  9781682820728 (hardback) | ISBN 9781682820735 (eBook)
Subjects: LCSH: Police misconduct--United States--Juvenile literature. |
  Police--Complaints against--United States--Juvenile literature. |
  Police-community relations--United States--Juvenile literature.
Classification: LCC HV8141 .D83 2017 (print) | LCC HV8141 (ebook) | DDC
  364.1/32--dc23
LC record available at https://lccn.loc.gov/2016013749

CONTENTS

A National Debate on Police Use of Force

In December 2014 President Barack Obama issued an executive order creating the Task Force on 21st Century Policing—a special commission of law enforcement officers, legal scholars, civil rights attorneys, and youth leaders. The task force was charged with making recommendations to America's state and local law enforcement agencies in order to "strengthen trust among law enforcement officers and the communities they serve," according to a White House press statement announcing its formation. The White House announcement also referenced "recent events in Ferguson, Staten Island, Cleveland, and around the country"[1] as reasons for why this executive order was necessary.

These "recent events" referred to by the White House were a series of incidents in 2014 that drew widespread attention, sparked a nationwide debate over police use of force, and led many Americans to question the level of trust they had in their local police. In Ferguson (a suburb of St. Louis, Missouri), Michael Brown, a teenager, was shot multiple times by a police officer and left for dead in the middle of a city street. In Staten Island in New York City, forty-three-year-old Eric Garner was choked to death by a police officer in the course of being arrested by group of police for illegally selling cigarettes. In Cleveland, Ohio, Tamir Rice, a twelve-year-old boy who was playing in a park with a toy gun, was fatally shot by a police officer responding to a dispatch call. None of the three victims were armed. Their untimely—and apparently unjustified—deaths because of police action created much public outcry, including protests and civil rights demonstrations.

Three Factors Driving Public Attention

There were several reasons why these three incidents sparked social unrest, inspired the creation of Obama's task force, and otherwise became part of a national conversation about police in America. One reason is the question of whether racial discrimination played a part in the deaths. In all three incidents, the victims were African American males, and the police officers who killed them were white. Some people asserted that these and similar incidents were simply extreme examples of how racial minorities have been abused by the police. The human rights group Amnesty International investigated police use of lethal force in a June 2015 report and concluded that "the shooting of Michael Brown in Ferguson, Missouri and countless others across the United States has highlighted a widespread pattern of racially discriminatory treatment by law enforcement officers and an alarming use of lethal force nationwide."[2] Both established civil rights groups like the National Association for the Advancement of Colored People (NAACP) and new ones such as Black Lives Matter have sought to address concerns about police abuses against black men and women.

Another reason why these incidents sparked nationwide concern is the police officers involved appeared to avoid any significant consequence for their actions. All three officers involved in the Brown, Garner, Rice killings were investigated by grand juries; all emerged unindicted and were thus relieved of being put on trial for their actions. Critics have argued that these cases are typical in that most police incidents of wrongful homicide or excessive use of force go unpunished. "There's shockingly little accountability for police and other law enforcement. . . . Indictments for police homicides are rare, and convictions almost nonexistent,"[3] writes journalist Jamelle Bouie. Suggested reforms to increase police accountability include the use of independent investigators to address complaints of police abuse and greater civilian oversight of police departments.

> "The shooting of Michael Brown in Ferguson, Missouri and countless others across the United States has highlighted a widespread pattern of racially discriminatory treatment by law enforcement officers and an alarming use of lethal force nationwide."[2]
>
> —Amnesty International, an organization that investigates and monitors human rights abuses worldwide.

Formed in 2012, the activist group Black Lives Matter has sought to draw attention to what it says is racial discrimination in the way white police officers across the country interact with African American citizens. Here, the group marches to demand justice for an unarmed African American teen who was shot by a white police officer in Madison, Wisconsin, in 2015.

The fact that many of these incidents have been recorded on video is a third reason why police conduct has become so widely seen and discussed. Bystanders with smartphones, for example, are able to record and transmit potential abuses to an Internet audience. The Garner incident was recorded and uploaded by a witness to his death. The Rice shooting was captured on a security surveillance camera, and this video was released on the Internet. The videos in both of these incidents have received millions of online views, furthering a national discussion. In response to the apparent value of video cameras as silent witnesses, some people have advocated that all police wear compact body cameras to record police-civilian interactions and thus possibly improve the conduct of the officers and even that of the civilians who then know they are being filmed.

Task Force Recommendations

Following several months of public meetings and deliberations, Obama's Task Force on 21st Century Policing released its final report in May 2015. Among its fifty-nine recommendations were for police to embrace a guardian mindset in the communities they serve, improve officer training on how to handle volatile situations, create a more racially and socially diverse workforce, and make internal procedures and investigations more transparent to the public. It also called for creating opportunities to promote mutual trust and understanding through more positive interactions between police and community members unconnected with law enforcement actions such as arrests and citations. In remarks to members of the task force when they presented a draft of their report, Obama said that "we have a great opportunity, coming out of some great conflict and tragedy, to really transform how we think about community law enforcement relations so that everybody feels safer and our law enforcement officers, rather than being embattled, feel fully supported."[4]

> "Indictments for police homicides are rare, and convictions almost nonexistent."[3]
>
> —Jamelle Bouie, chief political correspondent for *Slate*, an online magazine.

Whether or not the task force recommendations will help restore public trust in the police and resolve questions raised by the Brown, Garner, and Rice incidents (as well as numerous others) remains to be seen. Journalist Ted Gest notes that the localized nature of police in the United States limits the power of the president and the federal government to implement the fifty-nine recommendations. "In a country without a national police force and nearly 18,000 law enforcement agencies, many of which are local operations with only a handful of officers, there is no mechanism for forcing police to adopt agreed-upon best practices."[5]

Even as the task force's recommendations were being created and debated, Americans continued to be killed by police—almost twelve hundred people in the year 2015 alone. Regardless of how completely or quickly the Task Force recommendations are implemented, important questions surrounding the issue of police abusing their powers are certain to occupy the United States for years to come.

1 What Are the Facts?

Uniformed police officers in the United States are given broad legal powers to carry out their job. These include the power to use force, detain individuals, and even shoot and kill suspects under certain circumstances. However, these powers are constrained by laws, including the US Constitution. Recent incidents have led many people to believe that some members of the police force are abusing their powers—that they are using force (sometimes lethal force) against individuals without proper reason or legal justification. Research into the issue of police abuse of power is complicated by the fragmented nature of the American criminal justice system, different and evolving standards for what constitutes appropriate police conduct, and to some extent the lack of reliable nationwide data on police actions.

Police Powers and Responsibilities

There are about eight hundred thousand local police officers in the United States. Most are employed by one of eighteen thousand state and local law enforcement agencies. They are given significant responsibilities. Police officers are responsible for preventing crime, protecting people from criminals, maintaining order and public safety, enforcing laws, and providing emergency and other public services as needed.

Law enforcement instructor and author Fred M. Rafilson writes that "the fundamental purpose of the police force throughout America is crime prevention through law enforcement. To most citizens, the most visible representative of this effort is the uniformed police officer."[6] Their job is often difficult. Officers put their lives at risk. They are called to respond to urgent situations. In the words of legal expert Egon Bittner, police are commonly called to face "something that ought not to be happening and about which someone had better do something now!"[7] However, in addressing what "ought not to be happening," police often have to deal with people who are aggravated, upset, and often noncompliant. In some cases, they face determined resistance, threats, or even assault—part of why Jonathan Thompson of the National Sheriffs' Association calls policing a "dangerous, risky, hard, ugly job."[8]

In carrying out their responsibilities, police sometimes need to use force against others. For example, if police officers have reason to believe a person has committed or is committing a crime, they have the legal authority to place that person under arrest. If they witness a fight or a violent attack, they have legal authority to use force to protect themselves and others. Police are trained, equipped, and legally empowered to use force when necessary to do their jobs.

There is no universal definition of what constitutes a use of force, however. The International Association of Chiefs of Police defines force as the "amount of effort required by police to compel compliance by an unwilling subject."[9] Examples of force range from grabbing and restraining an individual to drawing a weapon and firing on that person. Police departments have policies governing what levels of force are justified in various situations. For example, police policy may authorize an officer to use physical holds against a person to make an arrest or defuse a situation but not authorize the use of a firearm to resolve the matter. Generally, lethal force is only authorized if the police officer believes the suspect was posing a significant and immediate danger to him- or herself or to others. Most controversies involving possible police abuse of powers involve whether officers reacted to a given situation with unjustified or excessive use of force.

Armed with Guns and Tasers

Many incidents involving use of force, both justified and unjustified, involve firearms or other weapons. In the United States, most police officers on patrol carry service revolvers or other handguns with them. Some police units, such as special weapons and tactics (SWAT) teams, use rifles and other larger weapons. Often in dealing with the public, these weapons remain secured or holstered, but if an officer deems it necessary to use force to resolve a situation, then he or she must determine whether a weapon

9

Police officers arrest a protester in Ferguson, Missouri, in 2014. Policing is a dangerous job because officers frequently have to deal with people who are aggravated, upset, or defiant, and peaceful protests can turn violent with little warning.

should be drawn and perhaps fired. Police recruits in America are required to undergo significant firearms training.

In addition to firearms, many police officers also carry and are trained in using nonlethal weapons that are meant to incapacitate or subdue people without killing them. Such weapons include baton sticks, pepper spray, and tear gas. In recent years a category of weapons called conducted energy devices, or CEDs, have been adopted by a growing number of police departments. Sometimes called stun guns or Tasers (a popular brand), these weapons use a painful electric charge to temporarily disable a target. A study by the Bureau of Justice Statistics (part of the US Department of Justice, or DOJ) found that the percentage of police departments who adopted Tasers and similar weapons rose from 7 percent in 2000 to 81 percent in 2013.

As with guns, police receive training before being authorized to use CEDs. While such weapons have been marketed as a nonlethal alternative to guns, there have been injuries and deaths associated with their use. In March 2014 in Miami, Florida, Israel Hernandez was "Tasered" by police while running away. The eighteen-year-old graffiti artist died of heart failure that the local medical examiner ruled was caused by a CED discharge. Law professor Donald E. Wilkes, Jr. and lawyer Lauren Farmer analyzed police and media reports of stun gun incidents and concluded that at least 618 deaths had been caused by police Taser use between 2001 and 2013. They argue that many CED incidents, including nonfatal ones, constitute "frightening abuses of authority and exercises of violent power."[10]

> "We have a profession with authority that no other profession has."[11]
>
> —Baltimore police chief Kevin Davis.

All of this equipment and training, as well as special legal powers and immunities, are meant to give police the option of using force as they deem necessary. "We have a profession with authority that no other profession has," Baltimore police chief Kevin Davis explained to reporters in July 2015. "We can take a person's freedom away and . . . a human life if justification exists to do so."[11]

Legal Limits to Police Powers

Although police have significant legal authority to use force and otherwise carry out their responsibilities, these powers are not unlimited. They are constrained by departmental policies and state, local, and federal laws. Police powers are also constrained by state constitutions and the US Constitution, which most police officers take an official oath to uphold.

The Fourth Amendment to the Constitution forbids "unreasonable searches" and gives individuals the right to be "secure in their persons." The Fifth Amendment protects people against self-incrimination (a person cannot be convicted based on a confession that may have been forced or coerced). The Fourteenth Amendment guarantees all Americans "due process of law." It is the job of the court system, with the US Supreme Court at its head, to apply the Constitution's general principles to cases involving police actions and to rule whether police have exceeded their lawful powers.

Several Supreme Court cases have dealt with police use of force, including lethal force. In the 1985 case of *Tennessee v. Garner*, Memphis police officer Elton Hymon shot Edward Garner in the back of the head as the fifteen-year-old was running away from a house he had burglarized. Hymon defended his actions by citing a Tennessee state law that authorized police to "use all the necessary means to effect the arrest"[12] of fleeing suspects. The Supreme Court ruled that this state law permitting lethal force to stop a fleeing suspect violated the Constitution. Instead, the justices ruled that lethal force was only permitted if police have "probable cause to believe that the suspect poses a significant threat of death or serious physical injury to the officer or others."[13]

Legal guidelines for police use of force were further developed in a 1989 case, *Graham v. Connor*, in which the court ruled that use of force against a suspect could be considered "objectively reasonable" by taking three factors into account: the seriousness of the crime at issue, the immediate threat the suspect poses to the safety of the police officers and others, and the extent to which the suspect is actively resisting or evading arrest. However, the court in *Graham* also ruled the "reasonableness of a particular force must be judged from the perspective of a reasonable officer on the scene, rather than with the 20/20 vision of hindsight."[14] For example, if in the heat of the moment a police officer thought he or she saw a suspect reaching for a gun, killing the suspect would be a reasonable use of force even if it turned out the suspect never had a gun.

Many people have observed that these two rulings—especially the *Graham* verdict—have in practice given wide latitude in allowing police the use of force. Civil rights attorney Chase Madar argues that by precluding hindsight or any second-guessing of what police officers believed at the time, "in actual courtroom practice, 'objective reasonableness' has become nearly impossible to tell apart from the subjective snap judgments of panic-fueled police officers."[15] While some say these standards are essential for officer safety, they make it difficult in practice for the legal system to rule certain uses of force excessive, even in cases involving lethal force.

Check Out Receipt

South Shore

Monday, January 22,
2018 2:24:14 PM

Item: R0446789793
Title: Do police abuse
their powers?
Due: 02/13/2018

Total items: 1

Thank You!

865

Police officers take an oath to uphold the US Constitution. Rights guaranteed to citizens under the Constitution include the right to be free from unlawful searches and seizures and the right to due process of law.

Journalist German Lopez writes that the intention of these decisions "is to give police officers leeway to make split-second decisions to protect themselves and bystanders. And although critics argue that these legal standards give law enforcement a license to kill innocent or unarmed people, police officers say they are essential to their safety."[16]

A Police Department's Use of Force Policy

All police departments have official policies defining what constitutes appropriate uses of force. The following passage is excerpted from rules governing the Denver Police Department.

The Denver Police Department recognizes the value of all human life and is committed to respecting human rights and the dignity of every individual, and the Constitutional right to be free from excessive force, whether deadly or not, by a law enforcement officer. The use of force, especially force likely to result in serious bodily injury or death (including a firearm), is a serious action. When deciding whether to use force, officers shall act within the boundaries of the United States and Colorado constitutions and laws, ethics, good judgment, this use of force policy, and all other relevant Denver Police Department policies, practices, and training. With these values in mind, an officer shall use only that degree of force necessary and reasonable under the circumstances. An officer may use deadly force in the circumstances permitted by this policy when all reasonable alternatives appear impracticable and the officer reasonably believes that the use of deadly force is necessary. . . . The calculus of reasonableness must embody allowance for the fact that police officers are often forced to make split-second judgments, in circumstances that are tense, uncertain, and rapidly evolving, about the amount of force that is necessary in a particular situation.

Denver Police Department Operations Manual, section 105.01, City and County of Denver, 2010. www.denvergov.org.

Recent Examples of Police Abuse of Powers

Controversies involving use of force have been debated in the public and in the courts for decades. However, in recent years there has been a steady drumbeat of news stories involving police brutality and police shootings that have garnered national attention.

One such example of excessive police force occurred on September 9, 2015, in New York City. Retired professional tennis player James Blake was arrested after he was mistakenly identified as a suspect in a credit card fraud investigation. A security video that was widely viewed online records a plainclothes white police officer, James Frascatore, running and tackling Blake, an African American, and slamming him to the ground. Frascatore, who had a past history of excessive force complaints, was suspended pending an internal police investigation. Some people argued that the while the mistaken identity was unfortunate, the officer was simply doing his job. But in October 2015 the Civilian Complaint Review Board, an independent New York City agency that handles complaints against police, concluded that while Frascatore may have had legal authority to temporarily detain and interrogate Blake, his use of force was excessive and constituted an abuse of that authority.

Another recent example of police force—this time lethal—happened on July 19, 2015, when University of Cincinnati police officer Ray Tensing shot and killed Samuel DuBose at a traffic stop concerning a missing license plate. Tensing initially claimed DuBose was threatening him with his vehicle; surveillance and body camera footage seemed to contradict his story. Tensing was indicted for murder and voluntary manslaughter and faces a possible prison sentence.

How Prevalent Are Excessive Force and Abuse Incidents?

The Blake and DuBose incidents are only two of multiple stories that have placed police abuse of powers on the national agenda. A question many have is whether these stories are an aberration or exception, or whether they are part of a larger pattern of police abuse of citizens—especially minorities. The question is hard to answer in part because the United States lacks a centralized or systematic data-tracking system that records police abuses, and police departments are often reluctant to voluntarily share such information to the public.

There are an estimated 45 million encounters between police and the public each year, out of which 12.5 million result in arrests. Richard Beary, president of the International Association of Chiefs of Police, argues that "what many don't realize is that the majority of contact law enforcement has with citizens is non-violent and non-controversial. . . . Of the millions of arrests police have each year, fatal encounters with law enforcement occur at a rate of far below 1%." He goes on to assert that "while any death or injury is, of course, regrettable, these incidents are rare; especially when you consider that many of the individuals arrested are under the influence of drugs and alcohol; have anger management issues; suffer from mental illness; or simply choose to be combative."[17]

However, others argue that recent publicity over incidents such as the DuBose case are lifting a veil from what they consider to be a serious problem of police abuse. Many argue that people in minority communities have long suffered from persistent abuses by police and that it is only now becoming an issue outside those communities due to the ubiquity of videos capturing specific incidents and spreading them online. "Black and brown people have been making these complaints for years, but they fell on deaf ears because no one wanted to believe that some officers would act that way,"[18] argues Cedric Alexander, president of the National Organization of Black Law Enforcement Executives. Other critics raise questions about whether abusive police are appropriately held accountable by police departments. Writer Bonnie Kristian cites a DOJ study that "revealed that a whopping 84 percent of police officers report that they've seen colleagues use excessive force on civilians, and 61 percent admit they don't always report 'even serious criminal violations that involve abuse of authority by fellow officers.'" This evidence of abuses going unreported leads her to conclude, "Police brutality is a pervasive problem, exacerbated by systemic failures to curb it." She adds, "That's not to say that every officer is ill-intentioned or abusive, but it is to suggest that the common assumption that police are generally using their authority in a trustworthy manner merits serious reconsideration."[19]

> "Police brutality is a pervasive problem, exacerbated by systemic failures to curb it."[19]
>
> —Bonnie Kristian, writer for the *Week* and the *American Conservative*.

Gaps in the Data

One problem in ascertaining the prevalence of police abuse of powers is the lack of national data. Most police departments are local; incidents of police use of force and other cases are generally investigated at the state and local level. Investigating trends in police brutality requires combing through thousands of local records. The 1994 Violent Crime Control and Law Enforcement Act requires the government to keep data about the use of excessive force by law enforcement officers, but more than two decades later, no national database exists. Some federal government agencies collect a few related statistics, but data is submitted to them from local agencies on a voluntary basis. For example, the DOJ surveyed the nation's police departments in 2013 asking them how often their police officers used force and under what cir-

A memorial shows a picture of Samuel DuBose, who was shot dead by University of Cincinnati police officer Ray Tensing during a traffic stop. Tensing was indicted for murder and voluntary manslaughter over the incident.

"The Talk" Black Parents Give About Police

Michele Sims-Burton is an African American Virginia resident. In this quote, she discusses "the talk" that she and other black parents feel compelled to give their children about the dangers they face when interacting with the police.

I have a 24-year-old son. I have given him the talk. . . . Ask the police before you reach for your license. Ask the police for permission to get your insurance card and registration out the glove box. Do not answer any questions. Just do as you are told.

Once my son and I were getting out the car at the shopping mall, the police approached him and asked him: "Did you just leave the mall?" I intervened. I instructed my son to "never, ever answer a question from the police." Ask the police: "Am I free to go?" Do not answer any questions. Be polite. Be cordial. But never answer any questions. Keep asking: "Am I free to go?" "Am I under arrest?" "What are the charges?" "May I make a phone call?" However, do not move suddenly. Do not get smart-alecky. Do not run. If the police start swinging, drop to the ground, protect your head and vital organs by curling up in a ball on your knees.

I've given my son this talk. And it terrifies me that in 2014, I text and call my son throughout the day not because I miss him so much, but because I am checking on his safety in this racist, militaristic society.

Quoted in Jazmine Hughes, "What Black Parents Tell Their Sons About the Police," *Gawker* (blog), August 21, 2014. http://gawker.com.

cumstances, but many departments did not respond or provided data that could not be compared with other police departments. "No federal agency comprehensively and reliably documents the use of force by police officers across the country," writes reporter Naomi Shavin. This lack of reliable data hinders getting answers to questions such as how often police use force, how often the force is excessive, and how often the force is lethal. "Short answer: It's impossible to know,"[20] concludes Shavin.

The FBI has announced plans to have more comprehensive nationwide data on police shootings and use of force incidents by 2017. However, the current lack of government data has caused private media outlets and organizations to tabulate their own counts of police shootings and other actions. The *Guardian*, a British-based newspaper, attempted to account for all police killings in the United States in 2015, including shootings, deaths of inmates while in police custody, and individuals killed by police vehicles. The number the *Guardian* came up for that year was 1,125. During the same year, the number of police officers convicted of crimes related to on-duty shootings was zero. Such a high number of deaths without any convictions for unlawful use of force has many critics wondering whether justice is being served.

> "No federal agency comprehensively and reliably documents the use of force by police officers across the country."[20]
>
> —Naomi Shavin, reporter for the *New Republic.*

Is Racism a Significant Factor in Police Misconduct?

On August 9, 2014, Michael Brown was shot and killed by police officer Darren Wilson in an incident whose details remain somewhat murky because of conflicting eyewitness accounts. The encounter began when Wilson stopped his vehicle to tell Brown to cease walking in the middle of the street. According to later investigations, there was a brief physical struggle between Brown (who was unarmed) and Wilson (still seated in his vehicle) during which Brown was shot in the hand. Brown then ran away a few yards and turned around, and Wilson opened fire again. Autopsy reports revealed six gunshot wounds, including two to the head. Wilson was suspended and resigned from the Ferguson police force; after hearing testimony from various witnesses (including Wilson himself), a grand jury declined to indict him on any criminal charges.

Brown, an eighteen-year-old high school graduate, was black, like the majority of his community of Ferguson, Missouri. Wilson, a twenty-eight-year-old five-year veteran of the Ferguson Police Department, is white, like most of the officers in the Ferguson police department. For many African Americans in Ferguson and elsewhere, the Brown shooting was yet another example of an unnecessary and tragic loss of young black man's life due to police action. Both the shooting in August and the grand jury's decision in November sparked massive protest marches and demonstrations led by civil rights groups, including the new group Black Lives Matter.

Both before and after the Brown killing, the issue of police brutality and police abuse of powers in the United States has been indelibly intertwined with the issues of race relations and America's treatment of minorities. Many of the recent attention-grabbing incidents, like the Brown shooting, have featured white police officers shooting or violently subduing black victims. Protests against police actions in Ferguson, Baltimore, Chicago,

Minneapolis, and other locations have often pitted minority populations against police departments and governments that are overwhelmingly white.

Members of Black Lives Matter and other critics of the police assert that their abuse of powers is of special concern for African Americans, and they contend that black men and women are at special risk for being unfairly accosted or even killed by police actions, more so than other Americans. These critics point to both individual racial prejudice held by police officers as well as what has been described as structural or institutional racism in arguing that police abuse of powers is related to racial discrimination. This analysis is not universally shared, however. Some people argue that race is not a determining factor in how police treat people and that police officers are being unfairly charged with racism.

Racial Disparities in Police Encounters

Michael Brown is far from the first or last black person to be killed by police. African Americans are statistically more likely to be arrested than other groups, are more likely to have force used against them, and are more likely to be killed in confrontations with police. What these disparities mean has been both studied and debated.

In 2014 reporters at the investigative journalism website Pro-Publica examined records of twelve thousand police homicides that were reported to the FBI. According to their analysis, from 2010 to 2012 white males ages 15 to 19 were killed at a rate of 1.47 per million individuals. From 2010 to 2012 black males ages 15 to 19 were killed at a rate of 31.17 per million—a rate 21 times higher than for whites. Given that blacks are a minority comprising only 6 percent of the population, for whites to be killed by police at the same rate as their black peers would require 185 additional fatalities over that three-year period. The journalists concluded that their "risk analysis on young males killed by police certainly seems to support what has been an article of faith in the African American community for decades: Blacks are being killed at disturbing rates when set against the rest of the American population."[21]

Other investigations have traced similar patterns. The publishers of the *Guardian* began a project to count all people killed by US law enforcement in 2015. By the end of June, the project (called "The Counted") had tallied 547 individuals who had been killed by gunfire or Taser use, were struck by police officers, or died in police custody. Of these, 154 were black. "When adjusted to accurately represent the US population," the newspaper reported, "the totals indicate that black people are being killed by police at more than twice the rate of white and Hispanic or Latino people." The *Guardian* went to note that "black people killed by police were also significantly more likely to be unarmed."[22]

> "Black people are being killed by police at more than twice the rate of white and Hispanic or Latino people."[22]
>
> —The *Guardian*, a British newspaper.

Racism May Not Be the Pivotal Cause

Some people have argued that these disparities are proof that race and racism are significant factors in how police treat minorities. Seen in conjunction with police incidents such as the Michael Brown shooting, these findings demonstrate that minorities may be especially vulnerable to police shootings and abuses of power. However, not everyone agrees with this analysis, arguing that there are important reasons—aside from racial bias—that explain these numbers.

Few people deny that the African American community has had a long-standing troubled relationship with the police. But some argue that American police—like American society—have changed much since the 1950s and 1960s when the civil rights movement was battling racial segregation. Police departments are no longer all white, racial discrimination in hiring is illegal, and open racism is no longer tolerated. The disparities in arrests and use-of-force incidents, according to some, reflect the fact that African Americans are more likely to be committing crimes and thus clash with police more than other groups. David Clarke, the elected sheriff in Milwaukee, Wisconsin, is prominent among those who frequently make these arguments. Speaking to Neil Cavuto at Fox News, Clarke attributed the higher numbers of blacks ar-

Marchers rally in Washington, DC, in the wake of the lethal August 2014 shooting of Michael Brown by police officer Darren Wilson in Ferguson, Missouri. Many African Americans viewed Brown's death as an example of the racism and brutality that African Americans across the country experience at the hands of white police officers.

rested and killed by police to the fact that blacks are more likely to be involved in crime, and hence are more likely to have risky encounters with the police. "The inconvenient truth here is that too often . . . the perpetrators [of crime] are young black males," he told Cavuto. In Clarke's view, criticizing the police for racism and incidents of abuse is unfair to the police, most of whom are simply doing their jobs and fighting crime. "Don't continue to use these very isolated incidents of police use of force and try to make it seem like that's the problem in America. The police aren't what's wrong about America."[23]

Clarke, an African American, has also presented his own story as an elected official as evidence that racism in both American society and American police departments is much less prevalent than in prior times. "We all know that race is an explosive issue in America . . . but white society has made great strides in trying to right that wrong. . . . I think I'm living testament to the fact that this country has changed."[24] To Clarke, his election and other

23

changes in the department and in the nation undercut arguments that police abuse happens largely because of racism.

Others have questioned the centrality of racism as a reason for police abuse by pointing out that black police officers have been involved in incidents of police abuse and brutality and that racism could not therefore be the major factor. For example, three of the six officers charged with causing the death of Freddie Gray (a Baltimore resident and African American who died while in police custody) were black. Journalist German Lopez notes that this "has led to some questions about whether racial bias is really at play—can a black cop be racist against his own racial group?"[25]

Overt Examples of How Racism Might Play a Part

Despite these critiques, many believe that racial bias still manifests itself in police department actions and may help explain why minorities may be disproportionately affected. Such racism may take the form of open racial prejudice that goes unpunished. But it may also manifest itself in subconscious biases and in systemic and institutional routines of police departments that victimize blacks more than others.

Evidence that at least some individuals in some police departments retain overtly racist attitudes and beliefs continues to trickle out, often in investigations of police brutality. In 2014 the DOJ investigated the Ferguson Police Department following the Michael Brown killing and subsequent civil unrest and found racist e-mails and other examples of police and city officials disparaging African Americans. Columnist Shaun King has chronicled similar incidents of racism in other police departments. In 2015, for example, a dozen San Francisco police officers were caught sharing racist text messages and were forced to resign. Several police officers in Fort Lauderdale, Florida, were caught sharing racist text messages and making a promotional video for the Ku

A young African American man is arrested. Experts say that law enforcement officers who are not overt racists may nonetheless be influenced by subconscious prejudices or thought patterns that lead them to treat members of different racial or ethnic groups inconsistently.

Klux Klan. Police chiefs in Oregon and Georgia were observed making racist comments and sending racist text messages to their coworkers. King argues that racial prejudice is at least partially responsible for police abuses of power and that any efforts to prevent police mistreatment of civilians must also address "the ever present realities of racism within our police departments."[26]

Implicit Racial Bias

When people argue that racial discrimination may account for some police abuse of power, most refer to incidents that go beyond using improper language in e-mails or texts. Police officers

Racism in the Police Force Is Institutional

Writer Albert Burneko argues that police shootings of blacks are not examples of American justice system failures but the system working as designed.

In August [2014], Ferguson, Mo., police officer Darren Wilson shot unarmed black teenager Michael Brown to death in broad daylight. That is what American police do. . . . Despite multiple eyewitness accounts . . . contradicting Wilson's narrative of events, a grand jury declined to indict Wilson. That is what American grand juries do.

In November 2006, a group of five New York police officers shot unarmed black man Sean Bell to death in the early morning hours of his wedding day. That is what American police do. In April 2008, despite multiple eyewitness accounts contradicting the officers' accounts of the incident, Justice Arthur J. Cooperman acquitted the officers of all charges, including reckless endangerment. That is what American judges do. . . .

The murders of Michael Brown [and] Sean Bell . . . and countless thousands of others at the hands of American law enforcement are not aberrations, or betrayals, or departures. The acquittals of their killers are not mistakes. There is no virtuous innermost America, sullied or besmirched or shaded by these murders. This *is* America. It is not broken. It is doing what it does.

Albert Burneko, "The American Justice System Is Not Broken," *The Concourse* (blog), December 3, 2014. http://theconcourse.deadspin.com.

(like all people) who are not overt racists may carry subconscious prejudices or thought patterns that might affect how they interact with members of different groups. Social scientists use the term *implicit bias* to describe automatic (even involuntary) ideas and associations that people have about certain groups. In a February 2015 speech, FBI director James B. Comey argued not only that many people "have unconscious racial biases and react differently to a white face than a black face," but that many police officers work in environments "where a hugely disproportionate percentage of street crime is committed by young men of color." After such experiences over time, even good police officers with the best of intentions "often can't help but be influenced by the cynicism they feel,"[27] says Comey. Social scientists have long researched how such subconscious thoughts may influence behavior. Implicit bias may especially affect behavior when emotions are heightened and split-second decisions are necessary—the

Racism in the Police Force Is Not Institutional

Attorney David French is a contributing writer to the *National Review*. He argues that racism is a vanishing phenomenon in American police departments.

Americans have been bombarded with assertions that black men face a unique and dangerous threat—not from members of their own community but from the very law enforcement officers who are sworn to "serve and protect" them. . . .

The conservative response is clear: While no one believes the police are perfect, on the whole they tend to use force appropriately to protect their own lives and the lives of others. Moreover, racial disparities in the use of force are largely explained by racial disparities in criminality. Different American demographics commit crimes at different rates, so it stands to reason that those who commit more crimes will confront the police more often. . . .

There are individual racist cops, and there are departments that will close ranks behind corrupt colleagues. But the chances of an innocent black man being gunned down by racist cops are vanishingly small. And that is good news indeed.

David French, "The Numbers Are In: Black Lives Matter Is Wrong About Police," *National Review*, December 29, 2015. www.nationalreview.com.

VIEWPOINT

conditions found in many police-civilian encounters and use-of-force incidents.

A series of studies in the early 2000s by psychologist Joshua Correll at the University of Colorado sought to study how police (and civilians) behaved by using a video game in which they had to make quick decisions as to whether to shoot people brandishing either a weapon or another object such as a cell phone. What Correll found was that people were quicker to shoot blacks with guns than whites with guns, more likely to shoot unarmed blacks than unarmed whites, and more likely to (mistakenly) refrain from shooting armed whites than armed blacks. In another study, UCLA psychology professor Philip Atiba Goff, showed people pictures of preteens identified as having committed a crime and asked them to guess their age. The study participants were far more likely to identify black children in the pictures as older teens or even adults than the white children pictured. The authors of the study argued that implicit racial bias tinged how people perceived the children. "Our research found that black boys can be seen as responsible for their actions at an age when white boys still benefit from the assumption that children are essentially innocent,"[28] said Goff.

To many observers, these and other studies show how subconscious biases can guide decisions and may account for police incidents such as the Michael Brown shooting or the November 2014 shooting of Tamir Rice. Rice, twelve, was playing with a toy gun in a public park when he was shot by police officer Timothy Loehmann. Loehmann, responding to a dispatch describing an individual waving a gun, shot Rice around two seconds after he got out of his police car. According to media reports, Loehmann thought that Rice was in his teens or older when he confronted him, thus perhaps perceiving Rice as a bigger threat that required a quick (and ultimately deadly) response. Whether implicit racial bias played a factor in the Rice and Brown incidents is hard to determine or prove on an individual case level. But former police captain Tracie L. Keesee argues that the fact that African American men are statistically more likely than men in other racial groups to be shot by police is in part due to the "the accumulation of unconsciously biased, often split-second, decisions."[29]

Environmental and Institutional Racism in Ferguson and Elsewhere

In addition to individual conscious and subconscious racial bias, some broader social realities and institutional practices within police groups may help create racial disparities in how police treat different groups. A good example of this was uncovered by the DOJ investigation of the city of Ferguson in 2014 following the

The Department of Justice, led by then–Attorney General Eric Holder (pictured), conducted an investigation into charges of racism within the Ferguson, Missouri, police department following Michael Brown's death.

Michael Brown incident. The DOJ actually conducted two investigations and produced two reports on the case. One focused on Officer Darren Wilson. It concluded that there was not sufficient provable evidence to file criminal charges against him. The other looked into the practices of the Ferguson police department and court system. Here the DOJ found ample evidence of various police abuses of power, often directed against minorities.

According to this report, Ferguson police officers routinely used excessive force against black suspects. Black motorists were more likely to be stopped and searched than white motorists, and they were more likely to be held in jail than whites. According to then–Attorney General Eric Holder, "Our investigation showed that Ferguson police officers routinely violate the Fourth Amendment in stopping people without reasonable suspicion, arresting them without probable cause, and using unreasonable force against them."[30] Police arrested citizens for talking back to them or recording them—a violation of the First Amendment. They routinely used Tasers in a dangerous and abusive way. Police officers were also encouraged by their leadership to detain and write multiple citations for minor violations in order to collect fines to raise revenue for the city.

The DOJ concluded that the brunt of police actions and abuses in Ferguson tended to fall disproportionately on African Americans. Almost 90 percent of use-of-force incidents were against blacks. Holder and the DOJ did not find a reason for these disparities apart from racial bias. According to Holder, "Our review of the evidence found no alternative explanation for the disproportionate impact on African American residents other than implicit and explicit racial bias."[31]

Is Ferguson Typical?

The DOJ report focused on one relatively small police department and leaves unanswered the question of whether Ferguson police abuses are typical in other police departments as well. Vincent Warren, a lawyer who has sued the New York Police Department for racial profiling, believes that the Ferguson report provides further evidence that "systemic, institutional racism exists in police forces throughout our country."[32] Barack Obama responded to the report by saying that it revealed a police department "systematically biased against African Americans in that city." He added that he believed that what happened in Ferguson was not a "one-time thing." However, he also asserted that it was not typical of police departments throughout the nation and that reforms, training, and other efforts can minimize racism and racial bias. "I think the overwhelming majority of law enforcement officers . . . have a really hard, dangerous job, and they do it well and they do it fairly."[33]

> "Systemic, institutional racism exists in police forces throughout our country."[32]
>
> —Vincent Warren, executive director of the Center for Constitutional Rights.

How Can Police Best Be Held Accountable for Abuses of Power?

On November 24, 2015, Chicago police officer Jason Van Dyke was formally charged with the murder of Laquan McDonald. Van Dyke, a white officer, had shot the seventeen-year-old African American sixteen times on October 20, 2014, in an incident that was captured by a video camera on another squad car. Many of the shots were fired after McDonald fell to the ground from the initial burst of gunfire. Van Dyke became the first police officer in Chicago in more than thirty-five years to be charged with murder for a work-related use-of-force incident.

At a press conference announcing the charges, state's attorney Anita Alvarez said that Van Dyke's actions "were not justified or the proper use of deadly force by an officer." She went on to say that "it's really important for public safety that the citizens of Chicago know that this officer is being held responsible for his actions."[34] Chicago mayor Rahm Emanuel stated that Van Dyke violated both "professional standards" and "moral standards" and that it was up to the justice system to hold him accountable. He explained that the officer's actions "are in no way a reflection of the dedication and professionalism that our police officers exemplify every day."[35]

However, the arrest and indictment of Van Dyke was not enough to pacify many people who were angry at the police department's actions. Over the next several days, thousands of protestors marched in street demonstrations. They were upset not only over the shooting itself, but the actions of the police department and the city following the incident. For example, McDonald's death was initially ruled a justifiable homicide hours after the incident, based on Van Dyke's testimony that McDonald was acting in a threatening fashion (testimony not supported by the dashboard camera, or "dashcam," video evidence). Van Dyke was not dismissed or fired but was instead assigned to paid desk duty while the department refused to release the video to the public for months after the incident. The department was accused of tampering with other video evidence; a Burger King manager said police officers asked to look at and then erased security camera footage from his nearby restaurant that recorded events leading up to the shooting.

This unfortunate incident was also not the only questionable mark on Van Dyke's record. The officer had fifteen prior complaints made against him for using racial slurs, pointing his gun without justification, and other unprofessional conduct. On one occasion in 2007, he was found guilty in a civil court of using excessive force during a traffic stop. The court awarded the victim $350,000 in damages, but Van Dyke was not disciplined by the police force, and he was allowed to keep his job.

For the protestors and other critics, the McDonald shooting was emblematic of a broader problem of police abuse of powers. That is, physical abuse and shootings of suspects are tragic occurrences that need to be addressed, but so, too, do the actions of fellow officers and departments that seek to cover up wrongdoing or excuse illegal behavior. Police departments are given the authority and responsibility to manage their workers and to investigate crimes, but many critics have argued that they have abused their power and position to shield police officers from accountability.

Internal Oversight Mechanisms

Officially, police departments are regulated by a variety of protocols and guidelines that, in theory, are meant to hold officers responsible for abuses of power. Some of these mechanisms are internal to the departments; others are external. All are meant to ensure that proper procedures are followed in order to maintain standards of conduct.

For example, police officers are supposed to file reports after arrests and use-of-force incidents explaining their actions, and these reports are supposed to be reviewed by their supervisors and commanders, especially in cases involving discharge of weapons. In addition to police accounts, civilians have the ability

Protesters and police face off during a rally in Chicago to protest the killing of Laquan McDonald, who was shot sixteen times by officer Jason Van Dyke. Van Dyke was later charged with first-degree murder in McDonald's death.

to provide alternative accounts and file complaints against the police. These complaints are usually investigated by the department itself; larger departments often have a specialized internal division to handle such complaints and investigate whether police officers abused their powers. After an investigation, a police department may issue a reprimand, recommend counseling or training, and in some cases discipline an officer with suspension or dismissal. Even if the complaint is ultimately not sustained by an investigation, it can remain in an officer's file. Most police officers receive no more than one complaint over their career. "In a properly run police department," argues lawyer Howard Friedman, "the fact that an officer has attracted a large number of complaints should trigger closer scrutiny."[36]

In serious cases in which an officer is suspected of committing a crime, the district attorney's office may step in and file criminal charges or seek an indictment from a grand jury. The step after indictment is trial. In such cases police officers are supposed to be treated just as any other criminal defendant. One example in which this process played out was the indictment, trial, and conviction of police officer Daniel Holtzclaw. In a clear abuse of police power, Holtzclaw had preyed on women he pulled over or otherwise encountered while patrolling an impoverished minority neighborhood in Oklahoma City. He used the threat of arrest, drug searches, and implied violence to coerce these women to perform sexual acts. After one victim complained to the police, an investigation was able to uncover the story. Holtzclaw was ultimately arrested and convicted on eighteen counts of rape and sexual battery.

> "In a properly run police department, the fact that an officer has attracted a large number of complaints should trigger closer scrutiny."[36]
>
> —Howard Friedman, private attorney.

Problems with Oversight and Accountability

However, many people believe that the Holtzclaw conviction is not the norm and that in practice, both police departments and local district attorney offices are too often not diligent in investigating and holding police accountable for crimes and abuses. Sid Willens, a lawyer, came to this conclusion when representing a client who was allegedly beaten by officers while in jail. The department's internal investigation simply accepted and repeated the officer's version of events as truth, dismissing the client's story. Willens argued, "It's like having the fox guard the chicken house."[37] Some statistical studies seem to support this cynical view. A 2007 study by University of Chicago law professor Craig Futterman examined records of 10,419 complaints against Chicago police for excessive force, illegal abuse, false arrests, and other abuses of power; he found that only 19 of those complaints led to a suspension from work of a week or more.

In 2004 the son of retired air force pilot Michael Bell was fatally shot in the head front of his Wisconsin home after a traffic stop. Bell was shocked by what he believed was a hasty and inadequate investigation, which took only forty-eight hours and cleared the police of all wrongdoing connected with the death of his son (also named Michael). "They hadn't even taken statements from several eyewitnesses," he stated. Although officers justified their actions by saying that they thought the victim had grabbed an officer's gun, "crime lab reports showed that my son's DNA or fingerprints were not on any gun or holster,"[38] said Bell. Despite the evidence that Bell's son was unarmed, which contradicted police testimony, the officers were exonerated. The Bell family received a settlement, but the officer who fired the bullet remained on the force.

Unwilling to let the incident go, Bell looked into historical records of police departments and commissions in Wisconsin and could not find a single incident in which a department ruled a police shooting unjustified. He says, "The problem over many decades . . . was a near-total lack of accountability for wrongdoing; and if police on duty believe they can get away with almost anything, they will act accordingly."[39] Bell took it upon himself to use part of a legal settlement from the shooting to put up billboards questioning whether police should be able to investigate their own officers for wrongdoing.

> "If police on duty believe they can get away with almost anything, they will act accordingly."[39]
>
> —Michael Bell, retired air force pilot and parent of a police shooting victim.

A lack of trust in the ability of police to police themselves may deter people from bringing complaints to law enforcement. In part, Holtzclaw was able to get away with his predations for as long as he did because his victims felt that the police would not be willing or able to help them if they complained. "I didn't think that no one would believe me," one of Holtzclaw's victim testified at a pretrial hearing on why she had not come forward. "I feel like all police will work together."[40] His victims were all impoverished minorities, many of whom had drug or prostitution records. This may have led him—and them—to believe that his word would be taken over theirs.

Another reason that outcomes such as the Holtzclaw trial are relatively rare is that police departments and district attorney offices often have a close working relationship in investigating and

Many critics say that police departments and local district attorney offices are frequently not as diligent as they should be in investigating complaints against police officers. All too often, they say, internal investigations accept the officer's statement as fact and dismiss any evidence that contradicts it.

prosecuting criminals. District attorneys need police officers to take part in prosecutions, and they also often rely on the support of police departments and police unions when running to be elected to their jobs. Some people believe these connections compromise the ability of district attorneys to go after police officers for abuses. "The DA [district attorney] relies on police officers as witnesses and investigators," writes Friedman. "This makes it politically difficult for a DA to prosecute a police officer."[41]

Independent Prosecutors and Civilian Review Boards

In addition to mechanisms and policies within the police department and local district attorney's office, there are possible outside avenues to follow in holding police accountable for excessive force or other abuses of power. These include special or independent prosecutors and civilian review boards. Some of these

VIEWPOINT

Special Prosecutors Should Handle Prosecution Cases Against the Police

Paul Butler is a law professor at Georgetown University and a former prosecutor in New York City. He argues that the close professional and personal ties prosecutors develop with police officers make it difficult for them to deal fairly with police who abuse their powers.

Like most lawyers, prosecutors are competitive and ambitious and the way you move ahead is to win your cases, and the way you win cases is get your star witnesses—the cops—to go the extra mile. All that makes it really tough to try to send one of them to prison—even when they have messed up big time. . . .

In a democracy, no one should be above the law. It's fine for citizens to profoundly respect the men and women who serve as law enforcement officers. But when those people break the law, they must be held accountable just like anyone else. The automatic appointment of special prosecutors in criminal investigations of police is the best way to avoid district attorneys' natural biases and make sure that justice satisfies the appearance of justice.

Paul Butler, "The System Must Counteract Prosecutor's Natural Sympathies," *New York Times*, December 4, 2014. www.nytimes.com.

alternatives rely on the cooperation of local police departments; others have the potential to overrule or pass independent judgments on department actions.

Independent prosecutors are attorneys not affiliated with local jurisdictions who are called in to handle particular cases, including cases of police misconduct. The process by which they are appointed varies from state to state and from case to case. Some states like New York vest power in the governor to appoint special prosecutors in police brutality and other cases. Other states place that discretion in the court system or the state attorney general. In Ohio, for example, the state attorney general appointed a special prosecutor to investigate the case of John Crawford, a black man shot by police in a Walmart (Crawford was holding a BB gun). In 2014, in part because of the activism of Michael Bell, Wisconsin passed a law mandating that all police-related killings be investigated by a state agency. Activists have called for similar laws in other states.

District Attorneys Can Handle Prosecution Cases Against the Police

Heather MacDonald argues that special prosecutors are not needed to bring police to trial; local district attorneys are fully capable of holding police officers accountable for incidents of brutality and abuse. MacDonald as a fellow with the Manhattan Institute, a conservative think tank based in New York City.

[In 1972] New York State created a special prosecutor to go after corrupt cops. [However], overzealous tactics by the special prosecutor led to convictions [against officers] being thrown out on grounds of entrapment and other misfeasance. . . .

Gov. Mario Cuomo eliminated the special state prosecutor . . . in 1990. [New York] City prosecutors have since proved themselves fully capable of prosecuting criminal cops and representing the public will. . . .

With regards to alleged police brutality cases, the record does not support the claim that local district attorneys stack the deck against prosecutions. . . .

It is wrong to blame the prosecutor when juries decide not to indict or convict an officer. That judgment represents the jury's understanding that officers' good faith decisions, made instantaneously in difficult circumstances, should be given the benefit of the doubt and not criminalized.

Heather MacDonald, "District Attorneys Have Shown They Can Prosecute Police," *New York Times*, December 4, 2014. www.nytimes.com.

Another mechanism to hold police accountable for excessive force and other abuses is the instituting of a civilian review board (CRB). CRBs are entities established by cities and are staffed by people (often appointed by the mayor or government officials) who are not police officers and are not subject to the police department's chain of command. Their purpose is to review police procedures and investigations and to receive and respond to civilian complaints against the police.

There are more than one hundred CRBs in various parts of the United States. Many were established in the wake of specific instances of police brutality or other abuses of power that community members and leaders believed were mishandled by police departments. The structure, function, and legal powers of these CRBs can vary widely from location to location. Some CRBs have their own staff of professional investigators separate from the police department, while others simply review the police depart-

With the police chief beside him, the Newark, New Jersey, mayor (right) announces the creation of a civilian review board in 2015. Boards such as this, usually made up of people who are not police officers, respond to civilian complaints about police.

ment's own investigations and conclusions. A few have power to discipline police officers, while others only have the power to make recommendations to the police chief or sheriff and/or the city or county's civilian leadership.

Whether CRBs have been effective is debatable. Some critics argue that these boards too often defer to police conclusions or do not have enough legal powers or resources to overcome cases in which police do not cooperate with them. Others contend that members of these boards may not appreciate the conditions police officers work in and the split-second decisions they are sometimes forced to make in tense situations. Jim Pasco, the national executive director of the Fraternal Order of Police, argues that "civilian review boards tend to, by definition, be made up of civilians who have no particular experience or insight into what went through that officer's mind."[42] Defenders of CRBs argue that effective ones can gain the trust of both police and community members. Willens helped found a civilian oversight authority in Kansas City in 1970, and he says that "once the cops got used to it, it worked, and it's still working, because what you're doing is simply trying to do what every business tries to do, [which] is get rid of the rotten apples. And there are very few overall."[43]

> "Civilian review boards tend to, by definition, be made up of civilians who have no particular experience or insight into what went through that officer's mind."[42]
>
> —Jim Pasco, the national executive director of the Fraternal Order of Police.

Federal Investigations

In some cases of police abuse, the DOJ has been brought in to do its own independent investigation and prosecution of police officers. Perhaps the most famous case of federal intervention occurred in response to the Rodney King beating. In 1991 four Los Angeles police officers were videotaped striking a prone King with their batons and kicking him for an extended time (King, an African American, had been pulled over after a high-speed chase). Four officers were indicted and tried for assault by the local prosecutor's office, but a jury declined to convict them—a development that led to several days of serious riots in Los Angeles, which claimed sixty lives. Then president George H.W. Bush invoked federal authority and had the case investigated by the DOJ. The four officers were then indicted and tried in federal court for civil rights violations, including violating King's Fourth Amendment protection from unreasonable arrest and his Fourteenth Amendment right to due process of law. In this trial, two of the four officers received convictions and were sentenced to time in prison.

Some observers believe the federal government should do this more often. However, a federal civil rights violation can be hard to prove in court. Prosecutors must prove that police officers willfully deprived someone of civil rights and acted with racist intent. For instance, the federal government declined to press charges against Darren Wilson for his 2014 shooting of Michael Brown, stating there was insufficient evidence to prove such intent. "You could say he was a bad cop," notes attorney Janet Johnson, "but it's hard to prove he acted only with evil intention of depriving Mr. Brown of his civil rights."[44] The higher legal hurdle has caused federal prosecutors to hesitate in bringing charges against police officers.

Should Body Cameras Be Mandatory for Police?

America's debate over police brutality has been inspired in part by incidents captured on video by surveillance cameras, by dashcams mounted in police cars, and by bystanders with smartphones. A growing number of police officers are also recording their actions with body-worn cameras—small, light, battery-powered cameras that can be attached to an officer's uniform, cap, or even sunglasses. Many interested parties have suggested these cameras should be part of the standard equipment for all police. Proponents argue that, by creating an audio/visual record, such cameras will not only help ascertain fault and hold either police or civilians accountable for encounters gone wrong, but may also reduce the frequency of such incidents. Others caution that body-worn cameras by themselves will not prevent police abuse of power and that their use raises thorny issues about privacy and unnecessary police surveillance of the public.

Increasing Support for the Use of Police Body Cameras

The exact number of law enforcement agencies in the United States using body-worn cameras that can record sight and sound is unknown but growing. Some estimates place the number between four thousand and six thousand. This number is changing as more and more police departments are evaluating the technology. Los Angeles and Milwaukee are two of the larger cities whose police departments are transitioning to the use of body cameras by the end of 2016.

Mandatory body cameras for police officers on duty have been recommended by many who have examined the issue of police abuse of power. The Obama administration has promoted their use. In announcing $20 million in federal grants for law enforcement agencies to obtain such cameras in September 2015, Attorney General Loretta Lynch said that "body-worn cameras hold tremendous promise for enhancing transparency, promoting accountability, and advancing public safety for law enforcement officers and the communities they serve."[45] Groups that have endorsed body cameras include the American Civil Liberties Union (ACLU), the Police Executive Research Forum, the US Conference of Mayors, and the civil rights group Black Lives Matter. Proponents argue that all three of the factors Lynch cites—transparency, accountability, and public safety—make cameras a useful method of addressing the problem of abusive police.

Transparency and Accountability

Transparency and accountability are closely related. Body cameras can potentially bring greater transparency to police-civilian interactions, revealing some of the details of events that otherwise would be left up to the recollections of the officers and civilians involved. One reason the 2014 Michael Brown shooting by police officer Darren Wilson in Ferguson, Missouri, has been controversial is that there is only one surviving eyewitness to the whole encounter—the police officer who did the shooting. Many Ferguson residents did not fully trust Wilson's recounting of events. Among those in support of body cameras is Lezley McSpadden, Michael Brown's mother, who in February 2016 urged the state legislature of Missouri to require their use, saying "This is not a black or white issue. This is a right and wrong issue."[46]

"Body-worn cameras hold tremendous promise for enhancing transparency, promoting accountability, and advancing public safety for law enforcement officers and the communities they serve."[45]

—Loretta Lynch, US attorney general.

The April 4, 2015, shooting of Walter Scott in South Carolina is another incident of police abuse of power that demonstrates how video can bring transparency and accountability to police incidents. Scott was pulled over in a traffic stop by police officer Michael Slager. Scott fled from his car and was chased and ultimately shot and killed by the police officer. In the moments immediately after the shooting and in his initial reports to his department, Slager characterized his shooting as self-defense, saying that after he tried to use his Taser to stop Scott, he and Scott got into a physical tussle in which Scott tried to forcibly take the Taser and use it against Slager. Attorney and writer Judd Legum, noting that police officers are very seldom prosecuted for on-duty shootings, said that the police department showed no sign of not believing him and that Slager "appeared well on his way to avoiding charges and pinning the blame on Scott."[47]

However, unknown to Slager, a bystander had captured video of the incident. The video, which was eventually released to media outlets, contradicted Slager's story. It showed Slager shooting a fleeing, unarmed Scott multiple times in the back from a distance of at least 15 feet (4.6 m). The video also showed Slager planting an object (possibly his Taser) next to the prone Scott. The footage drew national national attention. Slager was charged with murder in 2015. (In 2016 a federal grand jury charged Slager with violating Scott's civil rights and with obstruction of justice and unlawful use of a weapon during the commission of a crime.) Many observers believed that he would most likely have avoided

This still from a video shot by a bystander shows police officer Michael Slager shooting Walter Scott in North Charleston, South Carolina, on April 4, 2015. The video proved that Slager was lying when he said he shot Scott in self-defense and bolstered the argument that police officers should be required to wear body cameras.

Body Cameras Will Ensure Transparency

Richard E. Smith is the police chief of Wakefield, Massachusetts. He argues that body cameras can be an important step in increasing or rebuilding trust between communities and police.

In today's world, body cameras are the topic of many conversations on both sides of the issue. The reality is that cameras and recording devices are everywhere in our lives. Cellphone video clips are showing up daily, selectively reflecting the originators' position on issues. Surveillance cameras cover our streets, businesses, schools, and public places. Cameras worn by police are the next natural step. . . .

Most people, including juries, have no idea what today's police officer actually experiences and how he or she reacts. Testimony can recreate but cannot visualize the actual event. From the prosecutorial position, the body camera can present irrefutable evidence of fact. By utilizing body cameras, community trust and transparency can be increased or, if needed, built from the ground up.

Studies have shown that when body cameras are deployed, citizen complaints against officers drop measurably, as do unfounded complaints. Agencies that use body cameras have also seen a drop in use-of-force complaints.

Quoted in *Boston Globe*, "The Argument: Should Police Wear Body Cameras?," June 14, 2015. www .bostonglobe.com.

such charges and even kept his job were it not for the video. Accountability for Slager came from "the slimmest of chances that someone happened to be walking by with a camera," argued Cornell William Brooks, president of the NAACP. "That is an unsustainable proposition . . . it's time to put body cameras on the uniforms of police officers."[48]

Deterring Misconduct

Scott's shooting was an extreme case of police abuse, but many believe that it is not uncommon for police officers to concoct stories and rationalizations (alone or with their departments) to account for police shootings and cover up misdeeds. According to author Radley Balko, "Citizen shot video has now shown police to have lied or misstated the facts in countless incidents, including a number of fatal shootings."[49] Proponents of body cameras hope that such footage may serve both as a watchdog and a deterrent to such lying in the future. For example, police criminologist

Body Cameras Will Not Ensure Transparency

Radley Balko is a journalist and the author of *Rise of the Warrior Cop: The Militarization of America's Police Forces*. He argues that body cameras will not prevent police abuse and misconduct if police departments do not change policy to emphasize transparency and accountability.

Outfitting every police officer in the country with a body camera won't change much if those cameras don't come with policies that emphasize transparency. Cops who don't turn their cameras on when they're supposed to need to be punished. Video needs to be made available to the public, albeit with certain provisions to protect privacy. Video will certainly exonerate some officers accused of misconduct. But it will also inevitably show some officers to have lied, abused their authority, and broken the law. Building trust requires transparency in either scenario. . . .

Body cameras aren't a panacea. They're merely a tool. Unless elected officials impose the appropriate policies, any police culture determined to be opaque will figure out how to remain opaque, no matter what new technology is thrown its way. In a room with no light, even a thousand cameras can only record in the dark.

Radley Balko, "Police Cameras Without Transparency," *Washington Post*, August 21, 2015. www .washingtonpost.com.

Barak Ariel says the "police subcultures" that might condone police abuse and hide it from the public can by counteracted by the use of body cameras. "Police-public encounters," Ariel argues, "become more transparent and the curtain of silence that protects misconduct can more easily be unveiled, which makes misconduct less likely."[50]

In addition to providing transparency and accountability in police-civilian altercations, some argue that body-worn cameras may prevent such incidents by compelling better behavior among people (both police and civilians) who know their words and actions are being recorded. In 2012 a small police department in California put this idea to the test. Police officers in Rialto, a city of about one hundred thousand people, were equipped with body cameras and for a year were randomly assigned to two kinds of twelve-hour patrol shifts. In "treatment" shifts, the officers were instructed to wear and use their cameras to record all of their interactions with the public (with certain exceptions such as encounters with minors and informants). They were also required to inform those they encountered that their cameras were recording. In "control" shifts, police did not wear body cameras. Over the course of the year, all patrol officers were rotated among both kinds of shifts. Researchers found that when police officers worked in "treatment" shifts, they were half as likely to rely on use of force as when they worked the "control" shifts. Perhaps more remarkably, the total number of incidents involving police use of force declined 59 percent compared to the numbers of use-of-force incidents over the twelve months prior to the study.

In Rialto the number of civilian complaints made against police fell by almost 90 percent compared to the previous year. Some have speculated this drop in complaints might have happened because people realized they could not make up false stories about police abuse without being proved wrong by video footage. In this way body cameras have the potential to be a win-win situation both for police departments and for the general public, argues ACLU analyst Jay Stanley. "A lot of departments are finding that for every time they're used to record an abusive officer, there are other times where they save an officer from a false accusation of abuse or unprofessional behavior."[51]

Other communities have tried out body-worn cameras for their police officers and have reported results similar to those obtained in Rialto. Police in San Diego saw use-of-force incidents decline 46.5 percent and civilian complaints fall 40.5 percent after they began to use body cameras. A pilot program in which some officers in Florida's Orlando Police Department were equipped with cameras saw use-of-force incidents drop 53 percent and complaints fall 65 percent. Rialto police chief Tony Farrar helped design and report his department's experiment. He contends that the positive results measured stem in part from people (both police officers and the public) being aware that their acts are being watched and recorded. "When you know you're being watched you behave a little better. That's just human nature," Farrar contends. "As an officer you act a bit more professional, follow the rules a bit better."[52]

Police officer JaShawn Colkey displays the body camera she wears while on duty. Although advocates say all police officers should wear the cameras, critics raise a number of objections to the idea, including the cost of the cameras.

Even slight improvements in the self-control and behavior of suspects and police may be enough to defuse tensions and prevent encounters from escalating into abuse or violence.

Privacy Concerns and Other Policy Complications

These and other studies have created widespread interest in and support for mandatory body cameras for police. But questions have also been raised about the cost of equipping officers with cameras, what threats to privacy might be created both for police and the public, and what policies should be adopted regarding when cameras should be used and what should be done with the footage they create. Some critics argue that the effectiveness of body-worn cameras in preventing police abuse may be blunted by policies on how recordings are made and released.

One concern is how much discretion police have in actually using their cameras. Simply put, body cameras will not live up to their promise of transparency if police officers neglect to turn them on. There have been several publicized incidents of police shootings and complaints of abuse in which body cameras were never turned on or video footage mysteriously vanished. One example is the April 30, 2015, fatal shooting of Fridoon Nehad by San Diego police officer Neal Browder. Browder, a twenty-seven-year veteran responding to a call about a threatening individual with a knife, ending up confronting and shooting Nehad, a homeless person suffering from mental illness. Browder later claimed he fired because the person was walking toward him aggressively and Browder thought he was brandishing a knife (it turned out to be a pen). Browder did not have his body camera activated, contrary to department policy. He was not disciplined or held criminally liable.

Stanley argues that this and other incidents show that "policies and technology must be designed to ensure that police cannot 'edit on the fly'"[53] by turning off their cameras or erasing footage. One possible solution is to mandate that cameras be turned on through the entire police officer's shift. This removes the possibility of a police officer choosing not to record abuses committed on duty. But while ideal perhaps from a pure accountability perspective, continuous recording also raises "many thorny privacy issues,"[54] according to Stanley. It would create a massive intrusion into the privacy of police officers if it recorded all working minutes of their day, including chatting with partners during breaks or making private telephone calls.

Another approach would be to have police turn on the cameras when they are responding to a call or otherwise dealing with the public. This would minimize concerns about intruding on police officers' privacy. The San Diego Police Department, for example, has rules mandating that police officers record their law enforcement contacts; following the Nehad shooting, they expanded on the rules to require that police officers responding to radio calls turn on their cameras prior to their arrival. However, for such a policy to be effective, Stanley and others argue that there should be strong disciplinary policies in place for police officers who fail to turn their cameras on when they are supposed to. In addition, they argue that in cases in which video footage is lacking, people who allege police abuse should be given the benefit of the doubt. (In legal terms, there should be a "rebuttable evidentiary presumption" in favor of suspects and complainants in the absence of video evidence.) This would ensure that police departments would be more careful not to "lose" or fail to record encounters that might be the cause of a civilian complaint of abuse.

> "When you know you're being watched you behave a little better. That's just human nature."[52]
>
> —Tony Farrar, police chief in Rialto, California.

Who Sees the Videos?

Another concern over the use of police cameras is the question of who gets to see and control the video footage collected. For example, if officers are involved in a shooting or other use of force that results in a complaint or internal investigation, should the officers be able to see video of the incident before they write up their report or are interviewed by an internal investigator? Many people believe that previewing the video may give police officers an unfair advantage to spin their version of events. "I want to know that an officer's report, which is often taken as a true and accurate depiction of events, was not tailored to fit what is visible on the video footage," San Francisco resident Chelsea Ducote told the city's police commission at a hearing on camera policy. "I want transparency. I want accountability."[55] However, San Francisco district attorney George Gascón, a former police chief, has argued that giving police officers the ability to preview footage of incidents they are involved in would aid in their truthful recounting of what happened. "We want to give the officer an opportunity to have a full context of what occurred."[56]

Many police departments that have implemented body-worn cameras have maintained strict control over releasing videos to the public. The Los Angeles Police Department has classified all body camera footage as potential evidence that is not subject to legal open records requests. San Diego police chief Shelley Zimmerman, like other police chiefs throughout the United States, has repeatedly refused requests by the media and public to release body-camera footage of specific incidents, including police

An officer displays the camera attached to his uniform. To protect privacy, the LAPD has classified all body camera footage as potential evidence that is not subject to open records requests.

arrests of political protesters and police shootings. Balko argues that Zimmerman "wants the appearance of transparency that comes with body cameras, but she still wants her hand at the switch that controls the flow of information."[57]

Other police departments have more open policies regarding body camera videos. Some release body-camera video footage with restrictions (such as blurring faces) to protect the privacy of those filmed. The range of policies raises questions for many critics. Civil rights organizations have argued that all police departments should at least make police use-of-force footage available to the public and the press, and people who have been filmed (and their next of kin) should have access to footage in which they appear. The alternative seems to defy the point of having the body cameras in the first place. Or as Balko and others argue, if police are able to control the public release of videos, body cameras by themselves would do little to improve accountability and prevent possible police abuse.

Only a Tool

Body cameras can be valuable tools, many experts conclude, but cannot by themselves prevent police from abusing their powers or restore lost trust between police departments and the communities they serve. An anonymous police critic in Brooklyn, New York, argues that "body cameras don't address the real problem, which is police themselves."[58] But others argue that body cameras can be a first step to repair relations between police and communities where trust has been a problem. Inviting public input when creating policies on how body cameras and the video data they create are used is an essential step to ensuring that these tools are used appropriately. Barack Obama, in remarks on his police task force for reform, downplayed talk of "body cameras as a silver bullet or a solution." He argued that the decision to implement body cameras for police "has to be embedded in a broader change in culture and a legal framework that ensures that people's privacy is respected and that not only police officers but the community themselves feel comfortable with how technologies are being used."[59]

What Can Be Done to Prevent the Abuse of Police Powers?

Many reforms have been proposed and tried to prevent and reduce police abuse of powers, including police-caused fatalities. Some focus on how police are hired and trained; others involve alterations to police practices and procedures, including police discipline. Beyond advocating that police departments adopt new protocols, some proposals call for more federal government oversight of police. The ultimate goal of most if not all reforms is not only the reduction of police abuse, but a restoration of trust between police departments and those they serve.

Hiring and Recruiting Police

As stated, changing hiring practices is one typical reform measure. For example, Victor Hwang, a member of the San Francisco Police Commission, has called for his city to "revise its policies to encourage the hiring of officers who come from and live in the communities they serve."[60] Hwang and others argue that police officers as a group should be more representative of the places they patrol. If communities are racially and ethnically diverse, then police forces should reflect that diversity in hopes that systemic prejudices on the part of police forces will be neutralized and incidents of police brutality reduced.

Katherine Spillar, executive director of the Feminist Majority Foundation, offers another simple hiring suggestion to prevent police brutality: Recruit more female police officers. She points to studies made over the past forty years that consistently demonstrate that female police officers are far less likely to be involved in excessive force or police shooting incidents or be named in civilian complaints than their male counterparts. One reason, many believe, is that women officers tend to rely more on communication than on physical force when dealing with people and may be better at defusing potentially violent confrontations before they turn deadly. A commission interviewed Los Angeles police officers to examine problems following the notorious police beating of Rodney King in 1991; they reported that "many officers, both male and female, believe female officers are less personally challenged by defiant suspects and feel less need to deal with defiance with immediate force or confrontational language."[61]

Currently, females constitute between 12 percent and 18 percent of police officers, and many smaller police departments have very few female officers (and even fewer female commanders). Spillar argues that these numbers could improve by changing how police departments recruit job applicants. "Too many police recruiting campaigns feature slick brochures and billboards focused on adrenaline-fueled car chases, SWAT incidents and helicopter rescues—the kind of policing featured in television dramas and that overwhelmingly appeals to male recruits,"[62] she asserts. Such appeals may attract recruits (again, mostly men) who revel in action and displays of power—and may indirectly contribute to the

Some experts contend that police forces should reflect the diversity of the communities they serve as a way to reduce prejudice and incidents of police brutality. Here, an all-white group of police officers confronts a diverse group of protesters in the aftermath of a police shooting in Ferguson, Missouri.

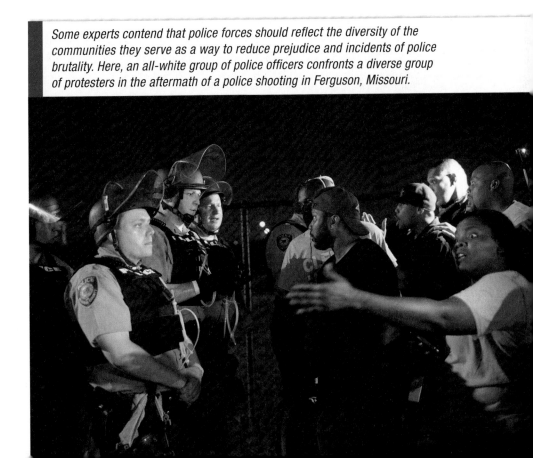

problem of police brutality. Spillar says that recruiting should instead stress the reality that most day-to-day police work involves service-related activities and nonviolent interactions. In other words, "the kind of policing that appeals to women,"[63] Spillar claims.

Police Training

Once people are recruited and hired, they need to be trained, both in police academies and later on the job. Many ideas for combating police brutality and abuse focus on police training and what kind of norms and expectations of police are being taught. Criminal justice professor Maria Haberfeld argues that police officers in America are simply not getting enough training. "An average training in the United States is fifteen weeks," she says. "Fifteen weeks is nothing."[64] She notes that police in other developed nations typically receive two or three times the amount of training that American police recruits do. And while some police departments provide continuing in-service training for police officers, the majority of police departments do not offer it, usually due to budget constraints. The result, she suggests, is an undereducated, undertrained police force that may be more prone to rely on shooting or using force when dealing with difficult situations or people.

Haberfeld and other critics see shortcomings not only in the amount of training police receive but in the police academy curriculum. Police training (both in-service and at academies) resembles military boot camps and often focuses on personal safety, firearms, combat techniques, and using physical force to subdue subjects. To Haberfeld and others, less-combative skills are neglected. Journalist Patrik Jonsson writes that, for example, "US police cadets spend an average of 58 hours at the gun range and eight hours learning how to de-escalate tense situations."[65] Critics argue that

> "US police cadets spend an average of 58 hours at the gun range and eight hours learning how to de-escalate tense situations."[65]
>
> —Patrik Jonsson, *Christian Science Monitor* reporter.

police need more training on how to communicate and interact with people, how to avoid or de-escalate confrontations, and how police actions (such as use of force) may impact the department's and officer's relationship with the community. "The majority of police officers are overwhelmingly trained with a focus on the technical part of use of force, and are not trained enough in the emotional, psychological, physiological aspects of use of force,"[66] says Haberfeld.

The Warrior Versus the Guardian

Some critics of police training say that such an emphasis on guns and combat is both a cause and result of police departments adopting a "warrior mindset." Some trace the roots of this mindset to law enforcement's ongoing "war on drugs," a set of policies and procedures that have turned many departments into paramilitary outfits conducting drug raids and other confrontational episodes with armed drug gangs. Other observers point to school shootings and to the September 11, 2001, terrorist attacks in America, which resulted in the federal government refocusing its efforts to protect American communities from terrorists and co-opting police departments as soldiers in a militarized campaign against terrorism. These trends, according to Jonsson, "hardened an already significant 'us versus them' approach by many especially urban police departments, where some parts of town feel, at least to cops, like war zones."[67]

Criminal justice professor and former police officer Seth Stoughton sees this mindset in much of the curriculum at police academies—an education that stresses the importance of physical safety for the officer and the need to be vigilant against a hostile world in which anyone is a potential killer. In this scenario, training conditions police officers to accept that their lives are always in potential danger. "As a result," Stoughton argues, "officers learn to treat *every* individual they interact with and *every* situation as a deadly force encounter in the making."[68] Such a mindset not only creates barriers to community policing but encourages officers to quickly use force if they feel they are being threatened or their authority is being questioned. It also reinforces, as Jonsson notes, an us-versus-them mentality in which police view their primary role as fighting, arresting, and killing criminal enemies.

By contrast, Stoughton and others (including the Task Force on 21st Century Policing) have called for a guardian mindset in which police see themselves as responsible for the safety and general well-being of the communities they serve. Susan Rahr, former sheriff of King County in Washington and a member of the task force, argues that although both soldiers and police officers are uniformed and armed, their missions are very different. She says:

> The soldier's mission is that of a warrior: to conquer. The rules of engagement are decided before the battle. The police officer's mission is that of a guardian: to protect. The rules of engagement evolve as the incident unfolds. Soldiers must follow orders. Police officers must make independent decisions. Soldiers come into communities as an outside, occupying force. Guardians are members of the community, protecting from within.[69]

Stoughton argues that police training can emphasize the guardian's role and teach police various ways to resolve situations without using force or abusing their legal powers. Some examples of types of trainings that go beyond learning how to handle guns and other weapons include nonenforcement contacts (training police officers to interact with people *without* any law enforcement actions such as ticket citations or arrests), de-escalation training (especially scenario-based training in which police officers role-play situations in order to learn how to manage volatile encounters), and informed training (reviewing real-life incidents in which civilian-police encounters went wrong or resulted in excessive force).

> "All officers responsible for abuses should be adequately disciplined and, where appropriate, prosecuted."[70]
>
> —Steven W. Hawkins, president of Amnesty International USA.

The Need to Weed Out Bad Cops

Some argue that changes in training and hiring will not do enough if there is inadequate police discipline. The surest way to reduce

President Barack Obama (left), flanked by Philadelphia police commissioner Charles Ramsey (right), addresses a meeting of the Task Force on 21st Century Policing, which has called for police to see themselves as responsible for the safety and well-being of the communities they serve, rather than viewing every encounter with a citizen as potentially life-threatening.

police abuse, in this view, is to thoroughly investigate such incidents and weed out officers who commit them. Steven W. Hawkins of Amnesty International USA, a human rights group, argues that all injuries or death caused by police use of force should trigger "a prompt, thorough, independent and truly impartial investigation" and that "all officers responsible for abuses should be adequately disciplined and, where appropriate, prosecuted."[70] But he and others contend that too few police departments in the United States live up to these seemingly obvious standards. Police departments too often belittle civilian complaints of abuse, take police officers' word in justifying their actions, or otherwise fail to hold bad officers to account. There has been a "systematic failure of police departments nationally to discipline officers who are found to have inappropriately engaged citizens and used excessive force," according to journalist Donovan X. Ramsey. He argues that the police reformers cannot ignore the "obvious fact

Police Should Be Public Guardians

Joseph Price was chief of the Leesburg Police Department in Virginia from 2000 to 2016. He calls for police to have the mindset of a guardian of their communities and to embrace smart policing to avoid excessive force.

Political leaders have put us in wars—the war on drugs, the war on crime, the war on terror, the war on gangs. . . .

We need to change that mindset, to teach officers that at times they may need to fight like a warrior, but most of the time they need to have the mindset of a guardian. A warrior comes in, takes over, does what he needs to do, and leaves. That's not what we want our cops to do. We want our cops to be part of that community and to solve problems—not for the community, but with the community.

Many inappropriate uses of force result from officers thinking, "I can't back down; I need to win at all costs." But that's not smart policing or effective tactics. We need to do a better job of training officers to control their adrenaline and try to defuse physical confrontations.

Quoted in Police Executive Research Forum, *Re-Engineering Training on Police Use of Force*, 2015. www.policeforum.org.

that police brutality is a national problem that persists, in part, because cops can get away with it."[71]

In addition to investigating officers after a shooting or complaint, Ramsey asserts that one way police departments can more actively ferret out problem officers is to use arrest reports and other internal data. A likely indicator of trouble is the number of times police charge people with "resisting arrest." Such charges are often made when police officers use force to detain individuals and are sometimes considered a potential red flag of police misconduct. "The logic," Ramsey argues, "is that an abusive officer will be more likely to cover up excessive force with the excuse that a suspect resisted arrest."[72] In 2014 the radio station

"Police brutality is a national problem that persists, in part, because cops can get away with it."[71]

—Donovan X. Ramsey, journalist.

WNCY combed through thousands of arrest reports of the New York Police Department and found that 5 percent of its police officers accounted for 40 percent of resisting arrest charges over the previous five years. One officer alone had made fifty-one such charges (a majority of New York officers had made none). It strains credulity, Donovan and others suggest, for these officers to be simply unlucky in the people they end up arresting. To critics like

Police Should Be Warriors

Dave Smith is a police trainer and a columnist for *Police*, a law enforcement magazine. He questions Barack Obama's Task Force on 21st Century Policing's assumption that police should see themselves as guardians instead of warriors, and he defends the warrior concept.

Recently, a Presidential Committee was formed to "fix" law enforcement. . . . The result was a hodgepodge of societal complaints about the law enforcement community, with the impressive title of "21st Century Policing". . . .

The first recommendation in this self-referential report is that the culture of policing needs to change. We need to become "guardians instead of warriors" because we have been teaching cops to be soldiers instead of protectors.

What? . . . Soldiers often make great cops since it is a natural transition from protecting a nation to protecting a neighborhood. I thought we all knew that already.

The warrior archetype is as powerful and important in our collective unconscious as any of the other "heroic archetypes," and until now I have never heard anything negative about it . . . the true root of warriorship is selflessness. . . . I would gladly have warriors protecting every community in this country and, in fact, I believe we do.

Dave Smith, "Warriors or Guardians?," *Police*, January 13, 2016. www.policemag.com.

Ramsey, it is more likely that this officer is a chronic abuser of police authority. Many argue that police departments should track and use such data to flag these officers, intervene with training and counseling, and if necessary, fire them before they create larger problems.

Reducing Police Abuse in Cincinnati

Although recent incidents centering on the issue of police abuse have caused major controversies in places such as Ferguson, Cleveland, and Baltimore, other communities have experienced crises in the past that have spurred them to adopt promising reforms. These examples may offer a path forward. One city many point to as a model of reform is Cincinnati.

Cincinnati's population of three hundred thousand is roughly evenly divided between white and black. That division became a talking point in 2001 when police killed Timothy Thomas, an unarmed nineteen-year-old African American, after a foot chase. Thomas was the fifteenth black person killed by police between 1995 and 2001. In the outcomes of the fifteen incidents, only one police officer had received as much as reprimand. Much like Ferguson after the Michael Brown shooting, Cincinnati erupted in four days of rioting in which residents expressed their profound distrust of the police. The police department was targeted by a private lawsuit as well as a DOJ investigation of its policies and past use-of-force incidents. Under both legal and social pressure, in 2002 the department settled the private lawsuit and reached an agreement with the DOJ in which it promised to enact a variety of reforms. These reforms have been credited with reducing police abuse and repairing relations between the department and the city's residents.

The DOJ's agreement with the police department mandated several drastic changes in its use-of-force training and other practices. The department was required to create a team of specially trained officers to respond to incidents involving mentally ill persons (one of the fifteen victims was mentally ill). Training was required on how to de-escalate confrontations. The agreement prohibited police from using choke holds, limited the use of chemical sprays and dog attacks, and required extensive documentation of all uses of force and critical firearms discharges (shootings meant to immediately incapacitate the target). The department was also ordered to create a system in which civilians could easily tender their concerns and complaints to the police.

Protesters rally in 2002 to mark the one-year anniversary of the death of Timothy Thomas, an unarmed black man who was shot to death by a white police officer in Cincinnati, Ohio. A subsequent investigation by the US Department of Justice led to a number of reforms that have been credited for mending relations between the police department and citizens of the city.

A citizen police review board was created to investigate, discipline, and fire police officers. The past pattern of a few bad actors escaping punishment was broken. "Police were actually held accountable,"[73] writes journalist Nicole Flatow. Police unions, long resistant to the firing of cops, came around to support the review board and other accountability mechanisms.

The reforms of the Cincinnati police department have not eliminated all police-related problems. Some residents still mistrust the police; complaints of abuse are still made. Police officers killed three black men in 2014. However, when those shootings occurred, there were no riots, in part because the police department was very open about what happened and what it was doing to investigate. It released the names of the officers involved and released dashcam video to the public. ACLU analyst Mike Brickner believes that not only have these reforms led to fewer incidents of police abuse in Cincinnati, when incidents do happen "police also have the tools and the training and the mutual understanding of how to talk about these issues . . . so that they can be quickly navigated through and done in a way that communities can agree on and live with and that they don't boil over in the way they did in 2001."[74]

What the Federal Government Can Do

Since 1994 the DOJ has been empowered to sue police agencies they find exhibit a "pattern and practice" of excessive force and other civil rights violations and to enter into legal agreements called consent decrees in which the DOJ mandates and monitors specific reforms. Some of the measures taken by Cincinnati police reflect such legally binding consent decrees. The DOJ has used these powers to investigate and reform other cities, including Seattle, Albuquerque, Los Angeles, New Orleans, and Oakland. These decrees, journalist Ramsey writes, have a record of effectiveness, but they are set for finite terms and only apply to individual police departments whose misconduct was bad enough to cause widespread complaints in the first place. Ramsey argues, "They are not the permanent, preventative, and national measures that are needed."[75] Ramsey and others have called for the federal government to establish national standards of what is acceptable police use of force and for increasing the DOJ's budget and staff to enable more continuous and routine oversight of the nation's eighteen thousand local police forces to ensure that police are not abusing their powers. "The prevalence of police brutality has long demanded federal intervention,"[76] says Ramsey.

However, some conservatives argue that the United States has a long-standing tradition of local government control over police forces and that the federal government's role should be strictly limited. "National police forces . . . have always been the hallmark of tyranny," argues journalist Alex Newman in opposition to what he views as efforts "to impose a national police force accountable to Washington, D.C. politicians and bureaucrats rather than local communities."[77] Disagreements over the relationship between the federal government, local police departments, and communities loom large over the ongoing search for solutions to the problem of police abuse.

Introduction: A National Debate on Police Use of Force

1. Office of the Press Secretary, "Fact Sheet: Task Force on 21st Century Policing," White House, December 18, 2014. www.whitehouse.gov.

2. Amnesty International, "Deadly Force: Police Use of Lethal Force in the United States," June 18, 2015. www.amnesty usa.org.

3. Jamelle Bouie, "Keeping the Police Honest," *Slate*, August 29, 2014. www.slate.com.

4. Office of the Press Secretary, "Remarks by the President After Meeting with Task Force on 21st Century Policing," White House, March 2, 2015. www.whitehouse.gov.

5. Ted Gest, "Will the President's Report Change American Policing?," Crime Report, March 3, 2015. www.thecrimereport.org.

Chapter 1: What Are the Facts?

6. Fred M. Rafilson, *Peterson's Master the Police Officer Exam*, 19th ed. Albany, NY: Peterson's, 2015.

7. Quoted in William H. Freivogel, "Why It's So Hard to Hold Police Accountable for Excessive Force," St. Louis Public Radio, December 7, 2014.

8. Quoted in Patrik Jonsson, "Amid Withering Post-Ferguson Critique, Police Around the Country Look Inward," *Christian Science Monitor*, August 9, 2015. www.csmonitor.com.

9. Quoted in National Institute of Justice, *Police Use of Force*, April 13, 2015. www.nij.gov.

10. Donald E. Wilkes Jr. and Lauren Farmer, "Electroshock Injustice: Fatal and Non-fatal Taserings by Police," *Digital Commons @ Georgia Law*, 2014, Paper 187. http://digitalcommons.law.uga.edu.

11. Quoted in Jonsson, "Amid Withering Post-Ferguson Critique, Police Around the Country Look Inward."

12. Quoted in Erin Fuchs, "These Are the Two Supreme Court Cases That Protect Cops Who Kill Unarmed Civilians," *Business Insider*, December 29, 2015. www.businessinsider.com.

13. Quoted in Fuchs, "These Are the Two Supreme Court Cases That Protect Cops Who Kill Unarmed Civilians."

14. Quoted in Fuchs, "These Are the Two Supreme Court Cases That Protect Cops Who Kill Unarmed Civilians."

15. Chase Madar, "Why It's Impossible to Indict a Cop," *Nation*, November 25, 2014. www.thenation.com.

16. German Lopez, "Walter Scott: What We Know About the South Carolina Police Shooting of an Unarmed Man," *Vox*, October 8, 2015. www.vox.com.

17. Testimony of Richard Beary Before the Task Force on 21st Century Policing, January 13, 2015. www.theiacp.org.

18. Quoted in Eliot C. McLaughlin, "We're Not Seeing More Police Shootings, Just More News Coverage," CNN, April 21, 2015. www.cnn.com.

19. Bonnie Kristian, "Seven Reasons Police Brutality Is Systemic, Not Anecdotal," *American Conservative*, July 2, 2014. www .theamericanconservative.com.

20. Naomi Shavin, "Our Government Has No Idea How Often Police Get Violent with Civilians," *New Republic*, August 25, 2014. https://newrepublic.com.

Chapter 2: Is Racism a Significant Factor in Police Misconduct?

21. Ryan Gabrielson, Ryann Growchowski Jones, and Eric Sagarra, "Deadly Force, in Black and White," ProPublica, October 10, 2014. www.propublica.org.

22. Oliver Laughland, Jon Swaine, and Jamiles Larty, "US Police Killings Headed for 1,100 This Year, with Black Americans Twice as Likely to Die," *Guardian* (Manchester), July 1, 2015. www.theguardian.com.

23. Quoted in Jessica Chasmar, "David Clarke, Black Milwaukee Sheriff: 'I'm Living Testament That America Is Not Racist,'" *Washington Times*, December 10, 2014. www.washington times.com.

24. Quoted in Chasmar, "David Clarke, Black Milwaukee Sheriff."

25. German Lopez, "How Systemic Racism Entangles All Police Officers—Even Black Cops," *Vox*, May 7, 2015. www.vox.com.

26. Shaun King, "An Annotated Guide to Racist Police Officers: More than a Few Bad Apples and Not Just in the South," *Daily Kos* (blog), September 8, 2015. www.dailykos.com.

27. James B. Comey, "Hard Truths: Law Enforcement and Race," Federal Bureau of Investigation, February 12, 2015. www.fbi.gov.

28. Quoted in American Psychological Association, "Black Boys Viewed as Older, Less Innocent than Whites, Research Finds," March 6, 2014. www.apa.org.

29. Tracie L. Keesee, "Three Ways to Reduce Implicit Bias in Policing," *Greater Good*, July 2, 2015. http://greatergood.berkeley.edu.

30. Eric Holder, "Attorney General Holder Delivers Update on Investigations in Ferguson, Missouri," US Department of Justice, March 4, 2015. www.justice.gov.

31. Holder, "Attorney General Holder Delivers Update on Investigations in Ferguson, Missouri."

32. Vincent Warren, "The Real Problem in Ferguson, New York and All of America Is Institutional Racism," *Guardian* (Manchester), December 4, 2014. www.theguardian.com.

33. Barack Obama, "Remarks by the President in Town Hall at Benedict College, Columbia, SC," White House, March 6, 2015. www.whitehouse.gov.

Chapter 3: How Can Police Best Be Held Accountable for Abuses of Power?

34. Quoted in Zach Stafford, "Tensions Rise in Chicago After Release of Video Showing Police Killing of Laquan McDonald," *Guardian* (Manchester), November 25, 2015. www.theguardian.com.

35. Quoted in Stafford, "Tensions Rise in Chicago After Release of Video Showing Police Killing of Laquan McDonald."

36. Howard Friedman, "Ways to Complain About Police Brutality and Police Misconduct," Law Offices of Howard Friedman, 2015. www.civil-rights-law.com.

37. Quoted in Martin Kaste, "Police Are Learning to Accept Civilian Oversight, but Distrust Lingers," NPR, February 21, 2015. www.npr.org.

38. Michael Bell, "What I Did After Police Killed My Son," *Politico*, August 15, 2014. www.politico.com.

39. Bell, "What I Did After Police Killed My Son."

40. Quoted in Jessica Tester, "The 13 Women Who Accused a Cop of Sexual Assault, in Their Own Words," BuzzFeed, December 9, 2015. www.buzzfeed.com.

41. Friedman, "Ways to Complain About Police Brutality and Police Misconduct."

42. Quoted in Kaste, "Police Are Learning to Accept Civilian Oversight, but Distrust Lingers."

43. Quoted in Kaste, "Police Are Learning to Accept Civilian Oversight, but Distrust Lingers."

44. Quoted in Terrell Jermaine Starr, "Why Don't the Feds Prosecute Police Brutality Cases?," AlterNet, August 29, 2014. www.alternet.org.

Chapter 4: Should Body Cameras Be Mandatory for Police?

45. Quoted in US Department of Justice Office of Public Affairs, "Justice Department Announces $20 Million in Funding to Support Body-Worn Camera Pilot Program," May 1, 2015. www.justice.gov.

46. Quoted in *New York Times*, "Michael Brown's Family Pushes for Missouri Body Camera Bill," February 17, 2016. www.nytimes.com.

47. Judd Legum, "Everything the Police Said About Walter Scott's Death Before a Video Showed What Really Happened," *ThinkProgress* (blog), April 7, 2015. http://thinkprogress.org.

48. Quoted in Tierney Sneed, "Why Body Cameras Could Cause More Problems than They Solve," *U.S. News & World Report*, April 10, 2015. www.usnews.com.

49. Radley Balko, "Police Cameras Without Transparency," *Washington Post*, August 21, 2015. www.washingtonpost.com.

50. Quoted in Stav Ziv, "Study Finds Body Cameras Decrease Police's Use of Force," *Newsweek*, December 28, 2014. www.newsweek.com.

51. Quoted in German Lopez, "Michael Brown's Family Said Police Should Adopt Body Cameras. They're Right," *Vox*, November 24, 2014. www.vox.com.

52. Quoted in Rory Carroll, "California Police Use of Body Cameras Cuts Violence and Complaints," *Guardian* (Manchester), November 4, 2013. www.theguardian.com.
53. Jay Stanley, "Police Body-Mounted Cameras: With Right Policies in Place, a Win for All," American Civil Liberties Union, March 2015. www.aclu.org.
54. Stanley, "Police Body-Mounted Cameras."
55. Quoted in Alex Emslie, "When Should S.F. Police Involved in Shootings Get to See Body-Cam Video?," KQED News, November 3, 2015. ww2.kqed.org.
56. Quoted in Emslie, "When Should S.F. Police Involved in Shootings Get to See Body-Cam Video?"
57. Balko, "Police Cameras Without Transparency."
58. Quoted in George Joseph, "Anti-Police Brutality Activists: Body Camera Guidelines No Panacea—and Might Make Things Worse," Intercept, May 15, 2015. https://theintercept .com.
59. Quoted in Wesley Bruer, "Obama Warns That Cop Body Cameras Are No 'Panacea,'" CNN, March 3, 2015. www.cnn.com.

Chapter 5: What Can Be Done to Prevent the Abuse of Police Powers?

60. Victor I Iwang, "Call for New Policing in San Francisco: Guardians Not Warriors," *San Francisco Chronicle*, February 8, 2016. www.sfgate.com.
61. Quoted in Katherine Spillar, "How More Female Police Officers Would Help Stop Police Brutality," *Washington Post*, July 2, 2015. www.washingtonpost.com.
62. Spillar, "How More Female Police Officers Would Help Stop Police Brutality."
63. Spillar, "How More Female Police Officers Would Help Stop Police Brutality."
64. Quoted in Paul Waldman, "Expert: U.S. Police Training in Use of Deadly Force Woefully Inadequate," *American Prospect*, August 27, 2014. www.prospect.org.
65. Patrik Jonsson, "Amid Withering Post-Ferguson Critique, Police Around the Country Look Inward."
66. Quoted in Waldman, "Expert."

67. Jonsson, "Amid Withering Post-Ferguson Critique, Police Around the Country Look Inward."

68. Seth Stoughton, "Police Warriors or Community Guardians?," *Washington Monthly*, April 17, 2015. www.washingtonmonthly.com.

69. Quoted in President's Task Force on 21st Century Policing, *Final Report of the President's Task Force on 21st Century Policing*. Washington, DC: Office of Community Oriented Policing Services, 2015.

70. Steven W. Hawkins, "Police Brutality Must Be Punished If We Want Real Justice for Michael Brown," *Guardian* (Manchester), August 14, 2014. www.theguardian.com.

71. Donovan X. Ramsey, "Want to Stop Police Brutality? Start Disciplining Officers," *New Republic*, February 10, 2015. www.newrepublic.com.

72. Ramsey, "Want to Stop Police Brutality? Start Disciplining Officers."

73. Nicole Flatow, "What Has Changed About Police Brutality in America, from Rodney King to Michael Brown," *ThinkProgress* (blog), September 11, 2014. http://thinkprogress.org.

74. Quoted in Flatow, "What Has Changed About Police Brutality in America, from Rodney King to Michael Brown."

75. Donovan X. Ramsey, "It's Time to Focus on the Other Fergusons in America," *New Republic*, March 13, 2015. www.newrepublic.com.

76. Ramsey, "It's Time to Focus on the Other Fergusons in America."

77. Alex Newman, "Obama Chooses Six Cities to Test Federal Police Scheme," *New American*, March 23, 2015. www.thenewamerican.com.

American Civil Liberties Union (ACLU)

125 Broad St.
New York, NY 10004
phone: (212) 549-2500
website: www.aclu.org

The ACLU is a national organization advocating for civil rights. It has investigated and published several reports on alleged police misconduct and abuse, which are available on its website.

CATO Institute

1000 Massachusetts Ave. NW
Washington, DC 20001
phone: (202) 842-0200
website: www.cato.org

CATO is a public policy research institute that believes in limited government. Its website has studies and commentary—sponsored by the institute—on police misconduct, militarization, and body cameras.

Fraternal Order of Police (FOP)

701 Marriott Dr.
Nashville, TN 37214
phone: (615) 399-0900
website: www.fop.net

The FOP is America's leading police union organization; it works on behalf of its members on all issues affecting police safety and other areas. It publishes the *FOP Journal*. Speeches, congressional testimony, and other resources relating to police issues are available on its website.

International Association of Chiefs of Police (IACP)

44 Canal Center Plaza, Suite 200
Alexandria, VA 22314
phone: (703) 836-6767
website: www.iacp.org

The IACP is a professional organization of law enforcement leaders that provides consultation, education, and research services to police departments nationwide. The association publishes the monthly magazine *Police Chief*.

National Police Accountability Project (NPAP)

499 Seventh Ave. 12N
New York, NY 10018
phone: (212) 630-9939
website: www.nlg-npap.org

The NPAP is a nonprofit membership organization of lawyers, law students, and legal workers dedicated to ending police abuse of authority through coordinated legal action and public education. The "Resources and Publications" section of its website has collected legal briefs, reports, and research papers on police misconduct and accountability.

Police Executive Research Forum (PERF)

1120 Connecticut Ave. NW
Washington, DC 20036
phone: (202) 466-7820
website: www.policeforum.org

PERF is a think tank that produces reports and recommends policies designed to improve community-police relations. Reports available from its website include *Re-engineering Training on Police Use of Force*.

Police Foundation

1201 Connecticut Ave. NW, Suite 200
Washington, DC 20036
phone: (202) 833-1460
website: www.policefoundation.org

The Police Foundation is a nonpartisan and nonmembership institute that conducts research projects on police activities and aims to improve the quality of police personnel and practices. Reports and infographics such as "When Can the Police Use Force?" are available on its website.

US Department of Justice, Civil Rights Division

950 Pennsylvania Ave. NW
Washington, DC 20530
phone: (202) 514-4609
website: www.justice.gov

The division has sued several cities for abusive police practices, and negotiated legal settlements requiring various police reforms. The text of those agreements, as well as other research and studies on policing, are accessible on the website.

Books

Radley Balko, *Rise of the Warrior Cop: The Militarization of America's Police Forces*. New York: PublicAffairs, 2014.

Robert J. Kane and Michael D. White, *Jammed Up: Bad Cops, Police Misconduct and the New York City Police Department*. New York: New York University Press, 2012.

Jeff Roorda, *Ferghanistan: The War on Police*. St. Louis: JCR Strategic Consultants, 2015.

Gerry Spence, *Police State: How America's Cops Get Away with Murder*. New York: St. Martin's, 2015.

US Department of Justice and Theodore M. Shaw, *The Ferguson Report: Department of Justice Investigation of the Ferguson Police Department*. New York: New Press, 2015.

Kristian Williams, *Our Enemies in Blue: Police and Power in America*. Chico, CA: AK, 2015.

Internet Sources

Matt Apuzzo and Sarah Cohen, "Data on Use of Force by Police Proves Almost Useless," *New York Times*, August 11, 2015. www.nytimes.com/2015/08/12/us/data-on-use-of-force-by-police-across-us-proves-almost-useless.html?_r=0.

Ronald Bailey, "Watched Cops Are Polite Cops," *Reason*, August 30, 2013. http://reason.com/archives/2013/08/30/watched-cops-are-polite-cops.

Harvard Law Review, "Considering Police Body Cameras," April 2015. http://harvardlawreview.org/2015/04/considering-police-body-cameras.

William F. Jasper, "Are Local Police to Blame?," *New American*, September 21, 2015. www.thenewamerican.com/usnews/crime/item/21557-are-local-police-to-blame.

Kimberly Kindy, "Thousands Dead, Few Prosecuted," *Washington Post*, April 11, 2013. www.washingtonpost.com/sf/investigative/2015/04/11/thousands-dead-few-prosecuted.

Shaun King, "Cops Who Kill Unarmed Victims—like Cedrick Chatman or Eric Garner—and Fail to Give First Aid Demonstrate Their Wanton Disregard for Human Life," *New York Daily News*, January 16, 2016. www.nydailynews.com/news/national/king-cops-show-no-remorse-victims-brutality-article-1.2499080.

Chase Madur, "Why It's Impossible to Indict a Cop," *Nation*, November 25, 2014. www.thenation.com/article/why-its-impossible-indict-cop.

Chris Mastrangelo, "The Face of Police Brutality," SocialistWorker.org, April 4, 2013. http://socialistworker.org/2013/04/04/face-of-police-brutality.

Michael S. Schmidt, "F.B.I. Director Speaks on Race and Police Bias," *New York Times*, February 13, 2015. www.nytimes.com/2015/02/13/us/politics/fbi-director-comey-speaks-frankly-about-police-view-of-blacks.html.

Rion Amalcar Scott, "The Etiquette of Police Brutality," *Crisis*, Winter 2015. www.asitoughttobe.com/2014/08/14/the-etiquette-of-police-brutality-an-autopsy.

Seth Stoughton, "How Police Training Contributes to Avoidable Deaths," *Atlantic*, December 12, 2014. www.theatlantic.com/national/archive/2014/12/police-gun-shooting-training-ferguson/383681.

John W. Whitehead, "Militarization Is More than Tanks and Rifles: It's a Cultural Disease," *Huffington Post*, May 21, 2015. www.huffingtonpost.com /john-w-whitehead/militarization-is-more-th_b_7336824.html.

Kevin D. Williamson, "No War on Cops, No War on Blacks: We Face Instead a Set of Conventional Intractable Systemic Failures," *National Review*, October 5, 2015. www.nationalreview.com/nrd/articles/424163/no-war-cops-no-war-blacks.

Nick Wing, "Here's How Police Could End Up Making Body Cameras Mostly Useless," *Huffington Post*, October 10, 2015. www.huffingtonpost.com/entry/police-body-camera-policy_us_5605a721e4b0dd8503079683.

Websites

Black Lives Matter (www.blacklivesmatter.com). Black Lives Matter is a network of civil rights groups that have organized and publicized various protests and actions against police abuses of African Americans and other civil rights injustices.

Cop Block (www.copblock.org). Cop Block is a website created by activists whose motto is "badges don't grant extra rights." It provides a place for individuals to share their stories and videos about experiences with the police.

Cop Watch NYC (http://copwatchnyc.org). Cop Watch NYC is a website to help citizens document police conduct and hold the police accountable.

INDEX